The Tadpole and the Frog

SUSAN KNOBLER

Adam & Charles Black London

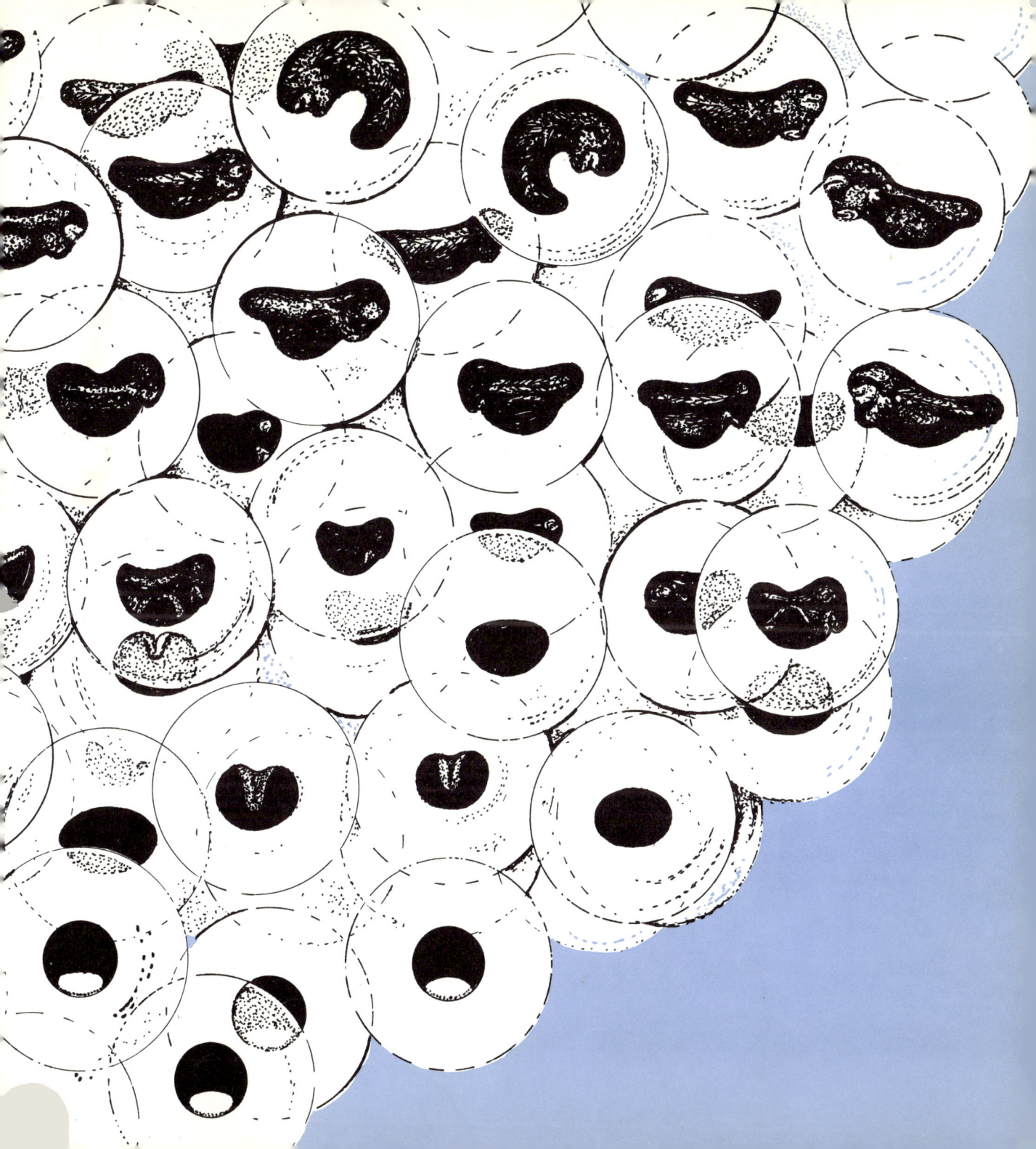

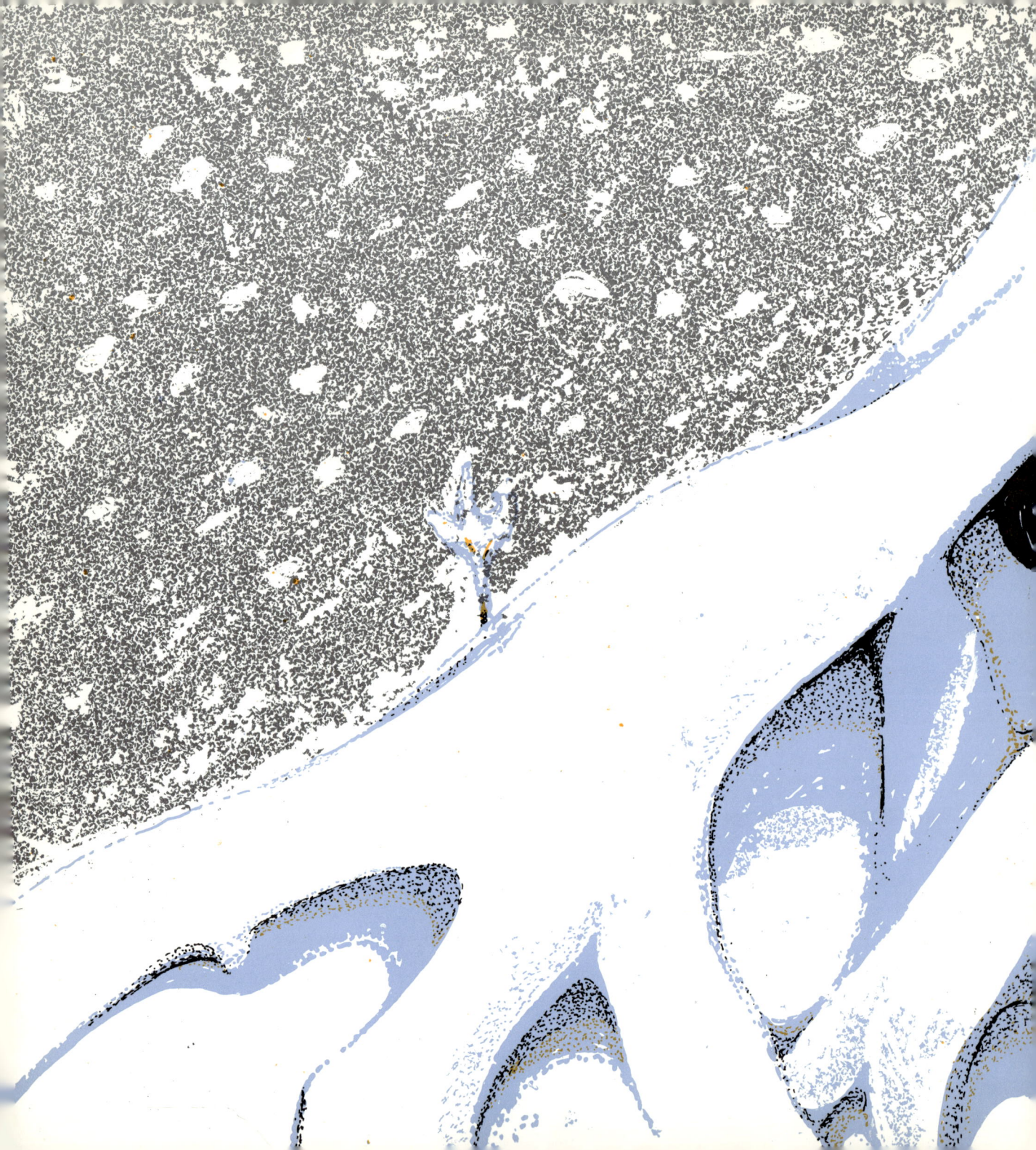

Reprinted 1977, 1981
First published in 1974
by A & C Black (Publishers) Ltd
35 Bedford Row, London WC1R 4JH

© 1974 A & C Black Ltd

ISBN 0 7136 1452 8

Colour reproduction and printing by
E T Heron & Co Ltd, Silver End, Witham, Essex